Eg[illegible]
elephants

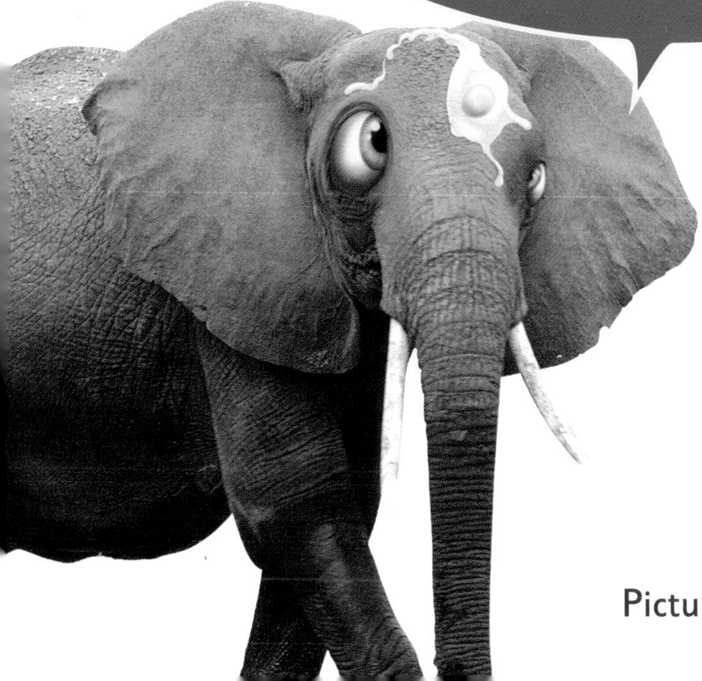

Words by Katy Pike
Pictures by Luke Jurevicius

An elephant

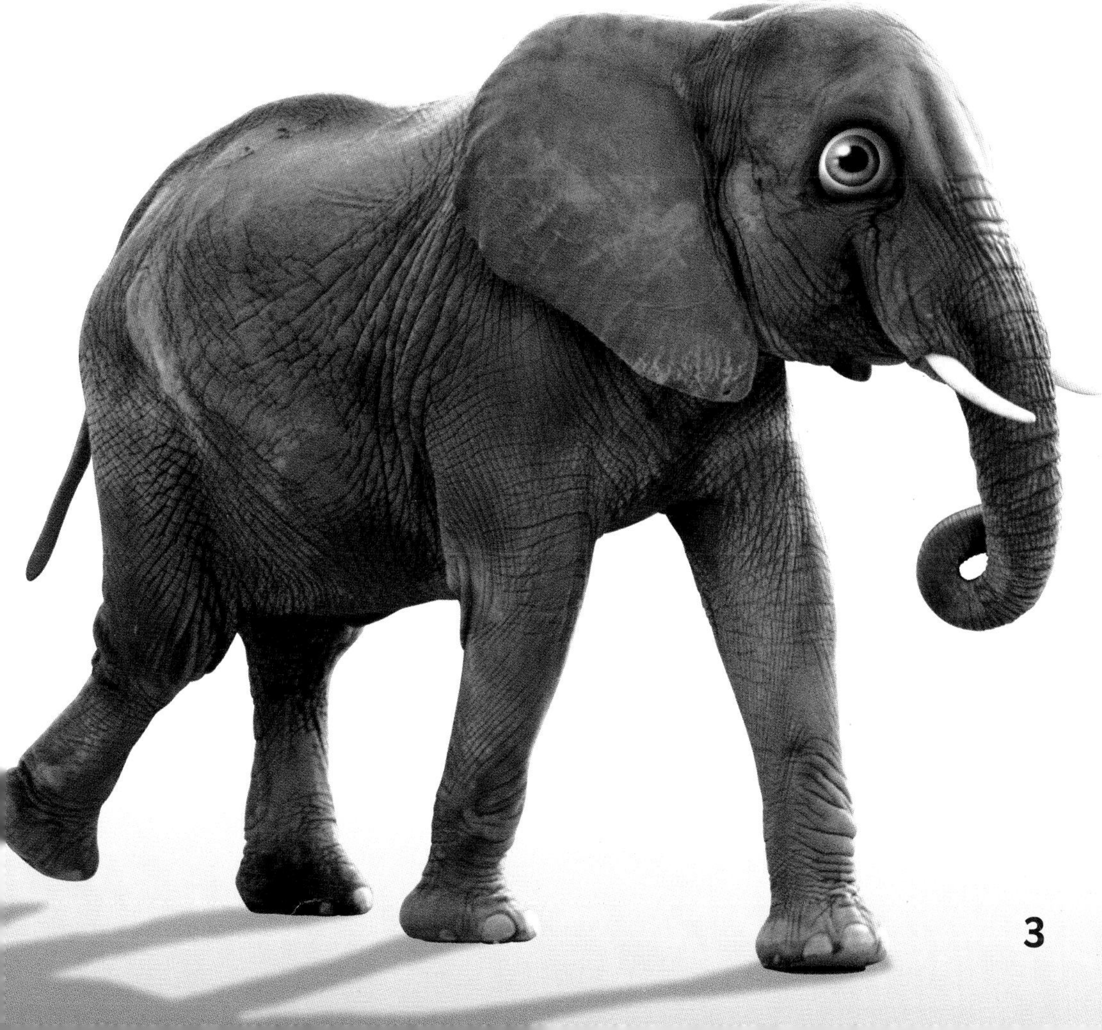

An egg for an elephant

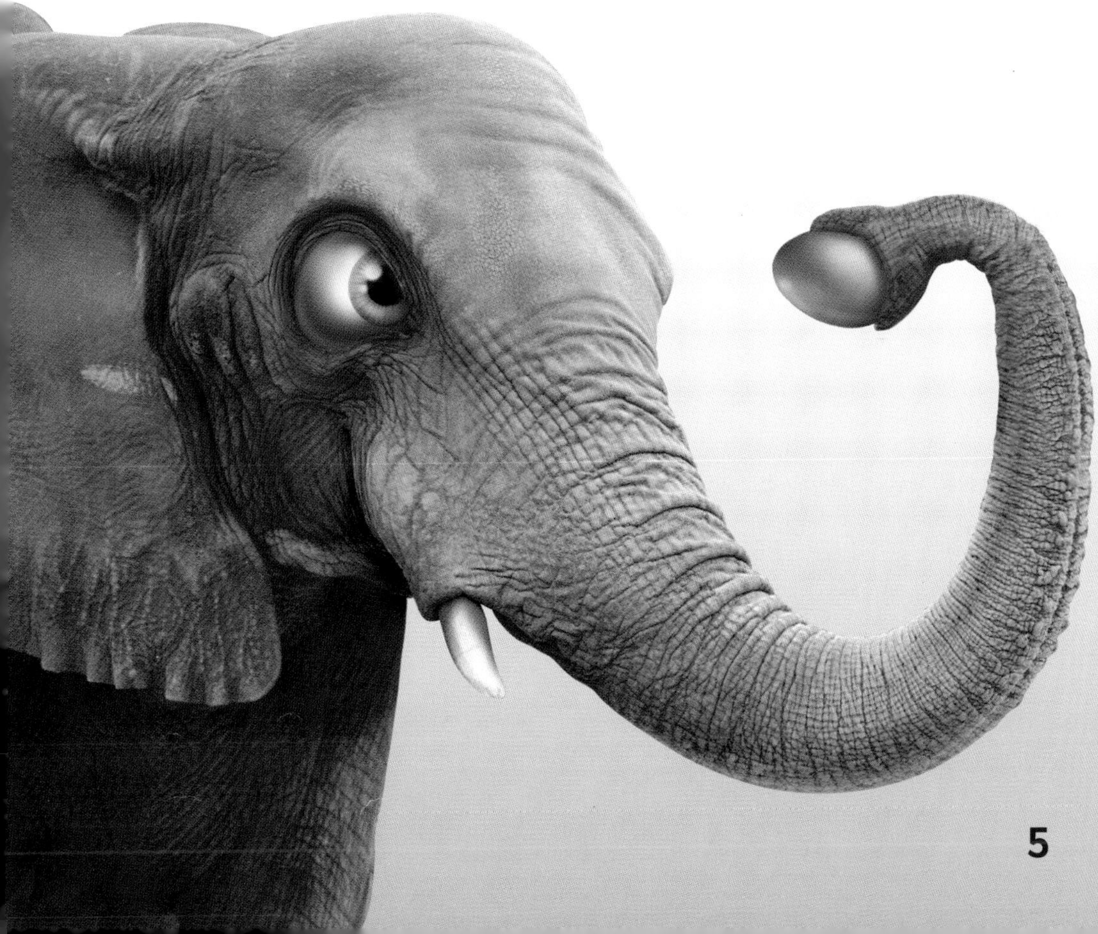

Eleven elephants

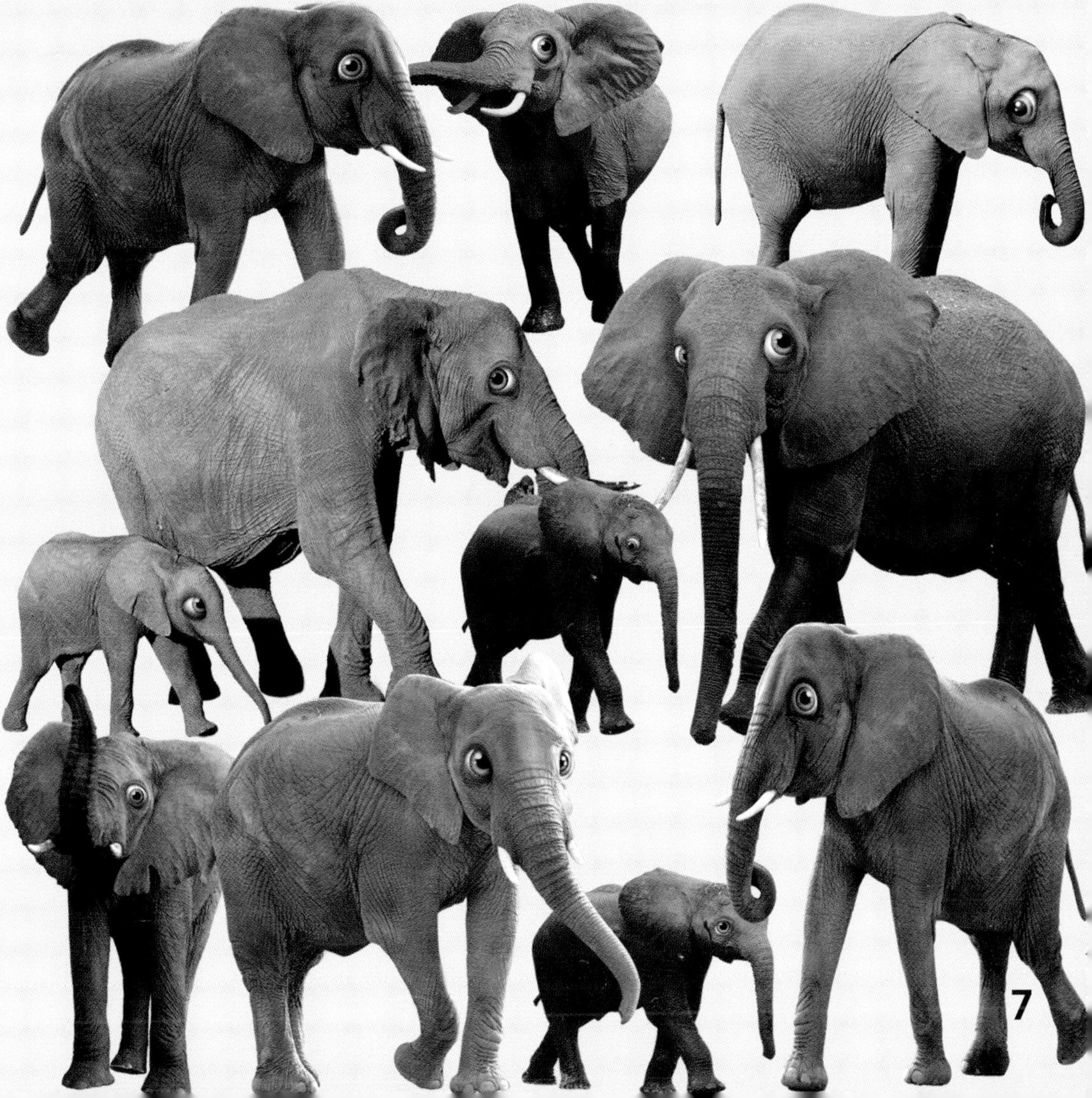

Eleven eggs

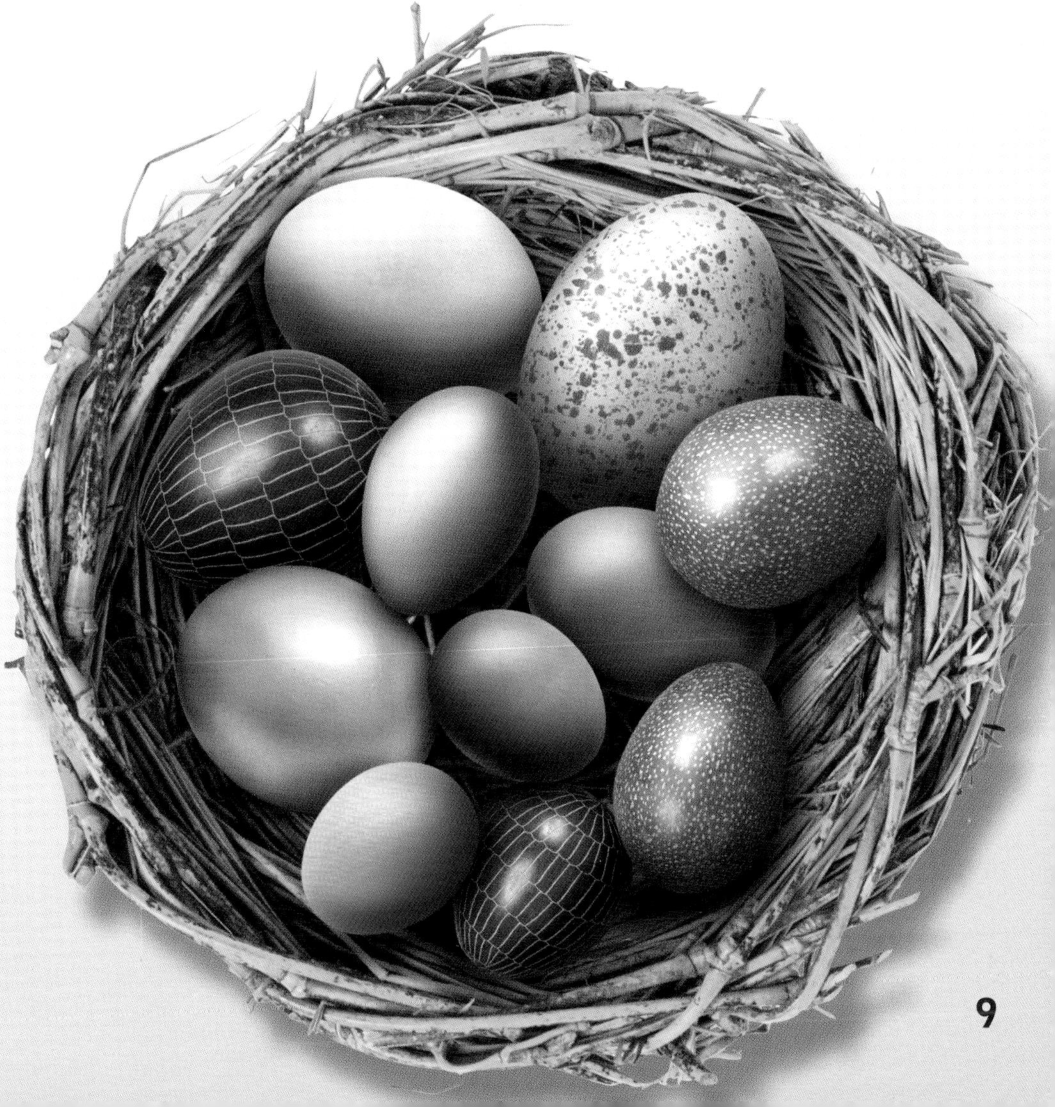

Do elephants have elbows?

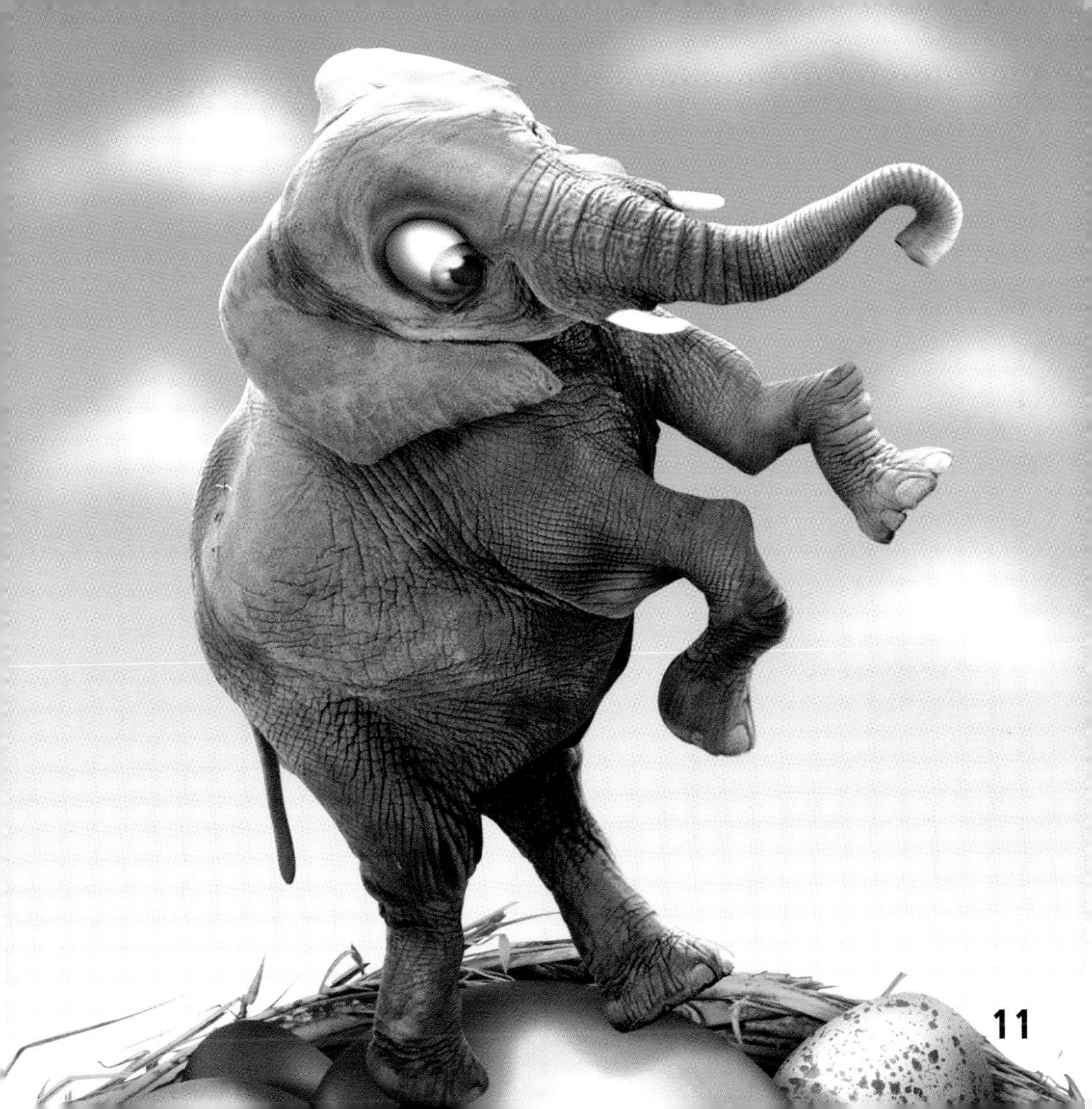

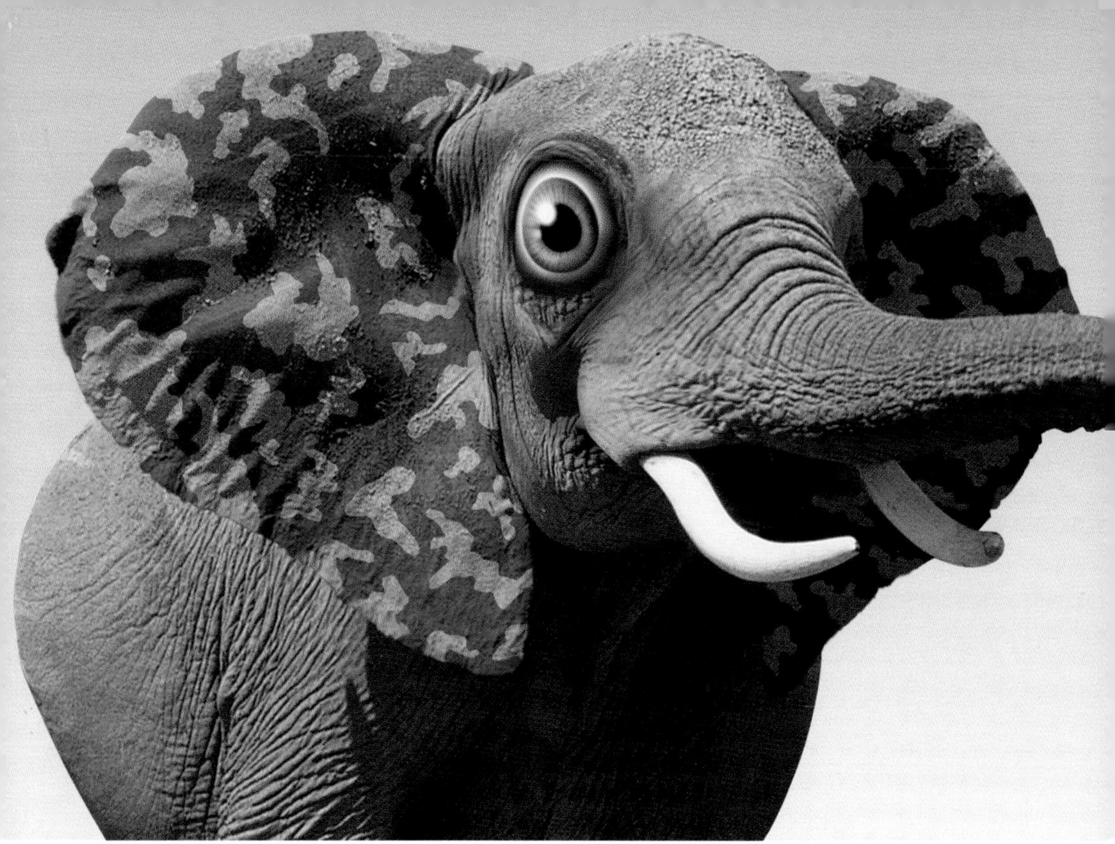

No!
Elephants have ears.